Magical Fairies *of* Molly Harrison

Featuring 25 illustrations for you to color, this fairy coloring book includes flower fairies and celestial fairies, mystical and playful.

© Molly Harrison All Rights Reserved
2015

www.mollyharrisonart.com

Printed in Poland
by Amazon Fulfillment
Poland Sp. z o.o., Wrocław